MAD OLSEN

All About Blitz Beer

Mad Olsen

ALL ABOUT BLITZ BEER

A Concise Guide

Translated by the Author

German Edition

© Mad Olsen: Rund ums Blitzbier (2014)

First Edition

March 2014

© Mad Olsen, 2014

Cover Art: © Jiuling Pasternak

ISBN-Nr. 978-1-291-80175-0

For Richard,

…who desperately wanted to know.

And Bobbo,

…a dear and solid friend for many years

Content

WARNING

This guide was written exclusively for connoisseurs, and friends of beer (herein referred to as "Beer Friends") respectively, with the purpose of clarifying a phenomenon whose closer inspection has long become overdue, and thus avoiding future uncertainty when applied.

All others, especially group beer drinkers, are dissuaded from buying this little compendium, especially if they are receiving medical treatment, suffering from circulatory disorders and stomach troubles, insomnia or other – above all psychical – trauma.

Claims on account of distinct deterioration of already existing and increasingly afflicting ailments asserted and magnified after perusal of this guide are strictly repudiated.

Preface for the English Edition

This book was originally written from a German point of view. More and more craft beer breweries have taken the stand against the big beer groups, the industry beer giants. This phenomenon can be witnessed in the United States too, and in Great Britain the CAMRA movement has had a tremendous success story.

Blitz beer is a term that has been discussed for quite some while. The uncertainty of what it actually is has led to severe misinterpretations, even on the Internet. As blitz beer also marks a kind of abyss between craft and group beers, it was the intention of the author right from the outset, to take the opportunity of giving an overview of what this term is, and is all about.

The craft beer recommendations given in chapter six are those introduced to the German readers, but may be interesting for others as well, since many beer connoisseurs make the purpose of a trip to Germany for this reason alone, and a lot of young up-and-coming brewers are from English-speaking countries studying the basics of brewing in Berlin, Germany. The author hopes that this little compendium will contribute something to the vast knowledge of beer in the world where English is spoken.

Mad Olsen, March 2014

Introduction

There is eco power and fast food, minute steak, daylight saving time … and blitz beer. Recently it has become something that more and more beer connoisseurs have started to take an interest in. Questions regarding blitz beer have become more imminent than ever before and only a few people have come up with reliable answers, but more than once, doubts have arisen as to whether the questions have been sufficiently clarified.

So, it was inevitable that voices were raised, loudly, and the true creator of this lovely expression was politely asked to unveil the secret once and for all to provide clarity, and with it, legal certainty for any man *and woman* whenever or wherever this expression shall be applied.

For those who only want to read the abbreviated version and save the time necessary to make oneself familiar with this little compendium, the annotation shall be made that the expression blitz (Blitz = Lightning for the uninitiated) beer has not been entered into Wikipedia (yet).

The decent beer connoisseur will have no choice but to read this little opus - which wants to come over as a first insight into the matter – especially, if he would like to answer many a question about blitz beer in a proper way. A spectre is haunting Europe – the spectre of blitz beer. Worry not, it is **not** dangerous.

Some will think of thunder and lightning and would rather have nothing to do with it. Others may think: Germany – blitz beer country? What? Where? Even women are being increasingly confronted with this expression by their men. "I'll only have a blitz beer quickly, and then I'll follow."

Blitz beer is a challenge which, of course, nobody has to accept. The beer friend should be in the picture and know what this is all about. It is difficult to say when blitz beer came about. It was definitely drunk before its name was coined (here), albeit unwittingly. It is probably quite safe to go back to the beginnings of beer brewing – right back to the ancient Egyptians – and this almost certainly may not be wrong.

It is easily conceivable that the architect of an Egyptian pyramid may have (totally innocently) said to one of his foremen at the end of the work day: "Let's have a quick beer before going home to our wives" and it is quite conceivable that he was thinking of blitz beer and/or that many a blitz beer had indeed been consumed.

Thus the term blitz beer has enriched the German beer landscape.

That 1984, of all years, was supposed to become the year that the term blitz beer came into this world, had not even been envisaged by George Orwell. Perhaps he had simply forgotten to take this phenomenon into account. By now this expression has reached greater dimensions, and demands a thorough scrutiny, one which is long overdue.

This is what is going to happen now. In order to answer as many related problems and questions, exactly, and in as much detail as possible, the author repeatedly carried out comprehensive surveys, asking interested parties, in order to find out which questions were really preying on their minds. Now… it's time to begin, and to cut a long story short: Here we go!

1 Origin

The term itself – Blitz beer in its gritty purity – was born in Prague. It remains somewhat unclear as to who the person was that uttered it "loud and clear" for the first time: the author, or his brother Tad.

"It so happened that Mad and Tad went on a beer trip to Prague over the weekend. The year was 1984 and the month December. The city was covered in snow, and there was certainly nothing more comfortable than sitting in a warm beer pub by the fire in which the famous Pilsner Urquell (in Czech *Plzeňský Prazdroj*) was served (which even today may be counted amongst the great pleasures in matters of beer tasting, outrageously good).

In those days Prague was still an integral part of the League of the Association of Eastern States and situated quasi "behind the Iron Curtain". The so-called Wessi was then converting the pint into pfennigs whilst the upright beer connoisseur from the East had to put some extra marks on the table as compared to being in his home country. Prague is still today the Mecca of the beer enthusiast.

"It was afternoon. As per usual, our train was to leave from the main station at about half past four. In those days, trains to Berlin would leave every seven hours and it would take them the same amount of time to reach their destination. At five to four we were still sitting at "Two Floors" (U Pinkasú) – or as on that very day of the unexpected coining of the word which we were not aware of – at U Flekú. Every beer connoisseur from the East, even if well advanced in years, knows that until the turnover U Flekú had been the traditional beer stronghold in Prague.

Here all and sundry would meet, as well as Heiner and Bodo from Munich. The place was always packed to the rafters. Officially there were no seats available anymore after twelve, but people moved closer together: Necessity was the mother of invention!

Nobody wanted to miss out on "The Black from the Fleck". It simply tasted too fantastic. (Then, because of the confined space, you were even allowed to step across the table if the "pressure" became unmanageable.)

"Anyway, it was five to four, and we were sitting in the first hall on the right (when you enter the pub), and we had had a few, perhaps ten. Our glasses were empty, and we watched the clock.

A waiter approached us with a huge tray full of Blacks, from the direction of the bar. We nodded, and one of us said: "Okay, let's have a blitz beer" and the waiter put two beers right under our noses.

"What was the idea of calling this a blitz beer right at that very moment? We did not need any comment. The main station was about two kilometers away. (According to Google it takes you about twenty-two minutes on foot.)

We still had exactly thirty-one minutes before the train departed. The streets were icy and slippery on account of the crusted snow. Not much time for a "blitz beer", because after that, it meant like stepping on the gas as if it were a matter of life and death.

We knew that nothing but a sprint was possible, and we also had to fetch our baggage from the locker. Not for the faint-hearted or slowpokes. When we appeared with our baggage on the platform, the doors of the train were being automatically closed. We waited until the train was starting, then opened one of the doors again (with those trains it was possible then) and jumped up as if we had all the time in the world. We were on the train. Not only was it worth having drunk a blitz beer, but it was also justified."

How is this term to be interpreted today against the background of its original application then?

At first, a blitz beer has an inseparable connection to an emergency. Briefly expressed: a beer in distress (an emergency beer), an explanation or term which can quickly lead one astray. An emergency only exists if an important event, scheduled before, is endangered in its execution without a real reason, apart from the pleasure of having an additional beer.

In order to carry out the execution of such an event even if the beer drinker would not like, or did not intend to abstain from having another one, then his sole means, which remains as a refuge, is to drink it as a blitz beer.

For lay people it means more or less to drink it down in one. But that is not mandatory as it comes down to a conscious ration of the amount of beer per time unit, i.e. how large the sip per second ought to be. Inexperienced blitz beer drinkers who overrate the danger of failing to realise their scheduled event often confuse blitz beer with "finish" beer, of which more later.

To get the hang of the right amount of beer, and time unit, an essential prerequisite is **the quality of the beer**. An inferior beer quality practically makes blitz beer drinking impossible. In such a case the talk is that the beer drinker guzzles the swill and then disappears *in a flash*.

Principally, the blitz beer drinker will not let it come down to the amount of beer he is about to drink, much less to the poor quality of a group beer. A blitz beer drinker is somebody who suddenly feels an unwanted disturbance. The pressure of approaching, pressing events which demand his presence, especially at a moment when he has no mind for them, in his private and cultural surroundings he feels compelled to do something he cannot delegate.

What remains is a smug blitz beer to allow oneself to contribute to the prolongation of the beauty of the atmosphere just a little longer. Experienced blitz beer drinkers also know the so-called "super blitz" and are able to execute it expertly, of which more later.

Summarizing, it shall be expressly pointed out that a *blitz* can only be consumed with pleasure. Enjoying one's beer is not a cliché. The hundreds of years that were necessary to deliver perfect craft beer quality must not be flippantly swept under the carpet.

To accomplish the perfect pleasure, for the beer connoisseur, has always been the noble aspiration of the true brewer. Pleasure can only be gained in an atmosphere of quietude, serenity and thoughtfulness: attributes which grace the true beer connoisseur, and which are conditions ipso facto to be able to master a blitz beer.

What, beer friends might object, could be the concerns? Namely if the *Prague situation* can automatically be applied to German conditions? The answer is simple: of course, not. It is impossible to imitate PU drinking in Germany.

First of all, this beer would have to be made available. (For Germany, the Czech brewery in Pilsen brews a "German" PU with more ABV and by doing so, unfortunately, with considerable quality loss.), but that is not the question. The Prague situation is only meant to show the prerequisites that the temporal pleasure of a blitz beer has to be measured against.

A beer friend does not have to be young and fit to be able to drink a blitz beer. Contemplated technically, it can also be had in a wheelchair. Important alone is the fact that one masters the time frame until the appointment, as this is the basis for calculating the time factor of your pleasure, and one should be aware that it will - depending on the state of health and mood – in most cases be different. However it sounds daft if someone announces that he has no more than sixteen minutes left and will, for that reason, and to be on the safe side, now start drinking a blitz beer.

2 Emergencies

This is especially for those who cannot imagine the requirements for an emergency. First of all, the emergency which led to the coining of the term is the model emergency which all emergencies will have to be measured against. In case of doubt, a committee of experienced blitz beer drinkers will have to decide whether the emergency to justify a blitz beer was real or made up. (Such a committee needs still to be set up.)

Often you may hear: "I must go home, my wife is waiting for me." Does this statement create an emergency to call one's beer a blitz beer? Basically, it needs to be said: The deciding factor is the overall conduct while enjoying beer! It is absolutely clear that such a laconic statement in the sense of a common declaration can impossibly constitute a blitz beer. In such cases the beer drinker has simply finished his consumption. To call one's last beer *afterwards* blitz beer is incorrect as it has not been announced as such time-wise sufficiently enough *in advance*.

An experienced beer friend would reach the conclusion that the speaker has *obviously* simply finished i.e. had his allocated beer consumption and henceforth terminated. A "finish beer" (as in "end of session" beer) also needs to be announced loudly and clearly for everyone to hear before its consumption. This indicates to one's beer friends that time is about to be run out, i.e. the countdown has set in, that all ideas communicated during important conversations are to be conclusively formulated or postponed for the time being.

This will appease all participants and also signal to those who have brought a bit more time to convince themselves that everything is still fine for them. This could also be understood as a noble thought of comradeship.

Here comes the all important question: Is it objectively possible to have a blitz beer after the finish beer? With a quiet conscience you may answer with "*yes*".

This however, is not what matters: crucially it remains whether there is, or not, – as a condition - an emergency, otherwise you would only be throwing your weight around. I have met beer friends who have claimed to have had one blitz beer after another, only because they had fallen in love with the expression. Of course, *none* of the beers they had had *was* in fact, a blitz beer.

More conscious beer friends, those with experience and considerable knowledge, asked me carefully, and beforehand, as to whether the beer they wanted to drink as a last one would be a blitz beer. Keen disappointment made itself at home when I negated that. Repeatedly I had to say that a "finish beer" never can be a blitz beer.

This is especially so if all the criteria for a finish beer have been clearly stated. This uncertainty led quickly to the fact that an opinion started spreading that only I, the author, had the right – or to be entitled – to a blitz beer.

This is nonsense, of course, but shows that the conscious beer connoisseur (max. three beers per day) can only get into a blitz beer situation on rare occasions. This does not go together. Emergencies are not planned.

What remains interesting is the fact that a blitz beer drinker will be looked at with special curiosity. Questions upon questions arise. Why does he get himself in such a situation? Does he have difficulties in dealing with time? Why does he make himself indispensable elsewhere? This makes it clear that enjoying beer does not, over a longer period of time, as at beer evenings, parties or a company "do" automatically justify a blitz beer but rather makes a mockery of it.

On the other hand, with such behavior, you will obtain infinite esteem by those who are in the know about the significance of a blitz beer and its application.

People often ask me: "Well, is this your blitz beer already?" or "Are you already at the blitz?"

At this point it should be added that experts in blitz beer matters call the blitz beer, "blitz" just that. This reveals the expert instantly. The blitz beer drinker and expert, as such, may also be addressed as "Blitzo". In a sociable party of beer friends, only one of the friends would usually be addressed as "Blitzo".

On another occasion I was asked the expert question as to whether a beer while being consumed can turn into a blitz beer.

Example: A telephone call forces the beer friend to down his bottle at once, which was expensive because of its extraordinary quality and difficulty to obtain. Can the beer now be called a blitz beer? Of course, not. On the one hand, a blitz beer has to be announced beforehand, too. On the other hand, the telephone call may have produced an emergency, but it was spontaneous, unknown beforehand, and led merely to the fact that the beer had been *guzzled* afterwards. There was quite simply no time to enjoy a blitz. The beer friend had been forced by a third party to drink up his bottle at short notice. A blitz beer can only be consumed on a voluntary basis and without restrictions, let alone under duress or by means of violence.

Generally speaking, having a blitz beer is a serious matter. After all, it is not a present. Many a joker asked me if it is possible to *start* with a blitz beer, as that saves the pressure at the end of the *session*. Such a question does not have to be answered. However, many a beer friend asks himself whether he will manage a blitz beer after his finish beer. Some of them cannot get to sleep at night for this very reason. Here it shall be stressed that you do not target a blitz. Nobody should put themselves under pressure, a blitz occurs unexpectedly.

For instance, I take a look at my watch in the middle of drinking and realize that I need to come to an end. In this moment the question arises: Still time for a blitz? Yes or no? My beer friends look at me anxiously and perk their eyebrows up.

What will be the outcome of his decision? He will certainly have no more than six minutes; otherwise he will miss the bus. Will he go for a blitz? If so, which sort of beer? ... and here comes the next deeply interesting question: What sort of beer suits best for a blitz beer? – Please find the answer in chapter six.

It strikes me as important that the blitz beer drinker knows his tolerance. This is not about the amount of beer he could consume within the hour but the span of pleasure construable in a minimum of time within which he will drink his beer without having to guzzle it. Blitz beer drinking is no athletic contest!

Will I be able to drink a pint within six minutes or will I have to take a small one to ensure that the pleasure will be upheld? In this case the sound mixture of experience and momentary condition will make the decision. It is conceivable that the decision was wrong. Example: I have decided to go for a small bottle of *Laguna* (.33l) but only needed half the amount of the remaining time to consume the beer in a decent way, completely addicted to the pleasure of it and without distractions of meaningless discussions. What now?

At this point the rarely executed super blitz beer gets a chance, shortly named *super blitz*. From the hitherto presented insights it becomes quickly obvious that a super blitz is rare because it requires enormous self-discipline and the already consumed blitz beer has extraordinarily sharpened the emergency by further narrowing the time gap which was not to be reckoned with under normal circumstances.

It is such a minimal time unit which can only be mastered by very experienced blitz beer drinkers. To be reminded: To enjoy is the centre point. The time gap suddenly emerged needs to be long enough to ensure the full pleasure of the beer.

Also the unpostponable commitment must not have ceased to exist. It is obvious – what you need in such a case is perfection. Therefore many a beer friend states quickly: "This is not my cup of tea." Which underlines: That requires extraordinary skills. That is also the point, the author is virtually pelted with incessant questions, "How do you drink a super blitz?"

"Is this a super blitz?" A short recap: A super blitz only emerges if you made the wrong choice of your blitz, be it that the bottle was a small one or the surprisingly quick, miscalculated drinking behavior during the blitz. What however, if the emergency was just simulated or changed by renegotiation (a telephone call) only to be able to brag in front of one's friends? "Yesterday I had a super blitz." Naturally, but what you will most likely hear is a condescending "Yeah, yeah. Sure you did..." instead of "Terrific, man! You've got it!"

Only a few experts can imagine the super blitz or intellectually understand it. The question should be: Was a super blitz necessary or had you better linger over the blitz a minute longer during the last sips?

Often the super blitz is used for shenanigans. One cannot repeat it or emphasize it enough; a super blitz does not come along easily. For many it is the repeated attempt to announce one's finish beer, but the real intention to do so is simply being procrastinated.

The super blitz is closely connected with the blitz. They form a dialectical entity, if you like, but seldom occurs. In some beer regions, like Berlin or Oslo, there is the opinion that in between is (must be) another blitz beer: the upper blitz. Blitz, upper blitz and super blitz, to put them in the right order. The reason for that goes back to assertions according to which, beer friends wanted to have had more than just one super blitz.

To prevent the super blitz from becoming a neat appendage to the blitz beer, it is generally agreed in some places that before the super there has to be an upper, or else it could easily degenerate into a daily sporting target for many a beer friend and by doing so not only undermine the sense of beer drinking in general but give this behavior, suspiciously, the appearance of a group drinker.

That would be a sacrilege which at any time beer connoisseurs know how to distance themselves from. (Here shall be added that there is no *mega blitz* after the super blitz. That would take the biscuit! …or be plain nonsense. Perhaps then we would also have the *ultra blitz* and the *hyper blitz*. Ha, ha! There would be no prospect of an end.)

How do I drink a super blitz (for conservative beer friends an upper blitz)? At first let us have a summary of all things which are of importance:

1)   An emergency constituted a blitz beer.
2)   An underestimation of one's own drinking behavior created "non-consumed" time.
3)   This "non-consumed or left-over" time should not be less than two minutes.

4)   Quick choice of a 0.33l or a half of quality
       beer for the super blitz.

Point number four shows that the choosing process must be executed without delay. Everything must happen now in the blink of an eye. The all important thing now is to keep calm, enjoy the beer within the remaining last three to two minutes and drain the bottle.

Occasionally, you can hear people saying: "I managed two super blitz beers last time." That borders upon bragging. Such utterances upset the beer friend and he does not listen. Bragging in this way is a mockery too. Amongst beer friends such behavior is unacceptable and undesired.

It is different if someone gives a credible account about a person he had met and whom he watched drinking a super blitz after a preceding upper blitz. He was, so to say, an eye witness. Such an account will not be heard very often. A second super blitz is not impossible. Mostly though, it is only said for fun.

Above all, uninitiated beer drinkers get a dizzying buzz in their head if one beer friend asks another loudly whether he has already started his super blitz, and a third throws in the remark that it could possibly be the second super. The uninitiated has little use for it and asks the beer friend carefully, who is just drinking his super: "Are you about to go?"

Basically, beer friends meet each other not only for the common pleasure of beer but also to take the meeting point into account, which is a site for exchanging ideas and viewpoints which one does not want to miss out on. As there is no schedule when beer is being enjoyed, and the decision to take part in the pleasure arrives often spontaneously and sometimes for oneself fairly unexpectedly, such a busy centre of encounter is characterised by a constant coming and going.

Many a beer friend hopes to meet this or that friend in order to exchange the latest information. Now it becomes clear that the newcomer asks his targeted interlocutor, who is in the middle of bliss, if he is just drinking his finish beer or perhaps even the blitz? As a rule, only experienced beer drinkers are accosted in such a way, but that is not interfering as it is a practiced routine.

An inexperienced blitz beer drinker when accosted responds somewhat insecurely in such a situation, or feels as if he is being made fun of. One should not forget that the common last beer which one would like to enjoy is a finish beer. "Let us finish for today." – "I'm finishing; I'll have to go home." – "But this is really my last beer now, I've already been here far too long." Altogether statements one will usually hear.

That means it is wrong to think that statements like "I'll have a blitz." or the invitation "Why don't you have a blitz?" have something in common with blitz beer. They are *de facto* false.

A typical blitz is revealed by the following example: You are expected at home by six, and not one minute later. ("Otherwise, the door is closed!") To be precise, the bus at 5:27 must not be missed. The bus stop is three minutes away (a quick pace already taken into account). The finish beer has been terminated. Your interlocutor's bottle is only half empty and the big hand has reached seventeen.

Right now at this point it is appropriate to say: "Okay, I'll have a blitz." In this very special case it would be justified to have a pint, let us say a *Mönchsambacher* (among connoisseurs affectionately called *Mönch* or *Monk*) if you focus solely on the pleasure, stop gabbing and are not a slowcoach. What happens if the bus is missed? Can you still claim later to have had a blitz, although the bus disappeared without yours truly?

A mishap like this clearly demands examination. The putative blitz beer came to nothing. The goal – the aversion of the emergency – was not achieved. What now? What has happened is called a blitz beer attempt. "I have tried it, but it was not meant to be." What one can state immediately is that such incidents cannot be dismissed out of hand. A bitter after taste lingers on. Above all from the echo of the consequences.

Courtesy dictates that those caught "red handed" at several blitz beer attempts are supposed to abstain from using the term blitz beer for a longer period of time. It would take away the blitz beer's content and definition. Otherwise all and sundry could at any time *try* a blitz beer. In the end the only beers we are drinking are blitz beers. What a mockery!

On the other hand, the arguments delivered so far underline that beer friends deal with the expressions of their consumed beers very respectfully. As already worked out, the real connoisseur tends to have a finish beer without ruffle or excitement, rather than try to take it up with the very strict requirements of enjoying a blitz beer. The idea of depicting the blitz beer expression in such a comprehensive way does not aim at teaching the mastering of a blitz beer as a challenge.

It is also not everybody's cup of tea, and it is important to know that this term should not be flung about like a pair of old socks. Actually, there are only a few beer drinkers who are able to really enjoy a blitz. This skill is mandatory if you want to show off in front of your friends, but in general, self-praise is discouraged. The beer shall be praised and not the skill of drinking it.

Blokes who already look like they have only guzzling in mind and who are not shy to openly demonstrate this, will not set much store in the skill of how to enjoy a finish beer, let alone start indulging in tirades about it. That is very much true for the beer tents in Munich every October where *drinking like a fish* becomes a popular virtue.

Here, terms like finish beer or blitz beer are immaterial and possibly even unknown. Guzzling is going on in the tents until the stanchions are bent out of shape. This has nothing to do with beer culture or pleasure, therefore no one in his right mind would start serving craft beer there. Would you cast pearls before swine? The beer friend stands aloof from these drinking contests with oompah music.

Normally he may have only been stranded there by chance, just once in his life - mostly by a false promise - and does not want to talk about that embarrassment or be reminded thereof. Such behavior is typical for group beer drinkers or attributed to people who do not know much about beer, of which more later.

3 Classifications

The beer connoisseur knows various classifications of beer. They are made according to applied criteria.

Blitz beer has the following classifications:

1 **Non-industrial beer**, also called **craft beer**: Beer of high quality using best ingredients in a highly refined brewing process. Beer for connoisseurs or simply called *beer*. Mostly brewed in small or medium-sized breweries. Stronghold: Franconia.

2 **Finish beer**: The beer which is usually drunk as the last beer of a satisfactory evening or conversation in a pleasant atmosphere, and which is supposed to signalise the end of one's beer consumption (until the next encounter).

3 **Blitz beer**: A beer which is consumed completely whilst upholding the full pleasure of its consumption under considerable time pressure because of an urgent appointment which cannot dispense with one's personal attendance, and without endangering the realization of the same (emergency beer).

4 **Upper blitz beer**: Has the same requirements as in point 3 whereas the time pressure has increased tremendously. Only possible if the available time for the blitz beer has surprisingly, not purposely, fallen below

the calculated span of time for its consumption. An upper blitz cannot be enforced.

5 **Super blitz beer**: Another term for upper blitz beer or the last possible progression of blitz beer, practically, after a twice failed attempt to fully use up the available time, originating spontaneously, whereas all criteria listed under point 3 keep their full validity. Only possible with low volumes, i.e. 0.33l bottles or halves. (Extremely rare.)

6 **Industry beer or group beer**: Alcoholic beverage named beer produced by corporations which call themselves groups from an economically profitable point of view, i.e. *Radeberger Gruppe*. Consumed by more than 90% of all beer drinkers worldwide.

Whilst craft beer breweries are further improving their production, exclusively in view of the palate of the beer connoisseur, group beer factories are trying to keep up with newly crafted beer varieties by using questionable recipes in their pseudo techniques. A much-quoted example turns around IPA (India Pale Ale), originally from England.

This type of beer which is relatively new in Germany and brewed by craft beer breweries has been brought to the market massively in recent times due to its huge demand. Now the groups are trying to close this void in their range of beers in their own way. Although the groups dismiss the craft beer breweries as unrivalled, they do remain a thorn in their side.

The dread that group consumers could find out that **beer is allowed to have taste** creates many a sleepless night among the group managers. The beer world of the group drinker would quasi change overnight (compare the situation in the U.S.), though it would cost him per beer a euro more. As long as the group drinker can be manipulated by low cent prices, his world will stay the same. But woe, woe betide…

It will need a *revolutionary situation* (group drinkers refuse to go on like this, the groups cannot help it anymore) if you want the conditions changed: two steps forward and (only) one back for a change, but as already told above: unthinkable in the foreseeable future. This should actually reassure the groups, unless the revolutionaries actually come from their own ranks. The group drinker will still have to bear his burden (in fact the burden of others) for quite some while.

Sure, also, beer friends have started on a shoestring. Meanwhile they have long since put this pediatric disease behind them. On the contrary: They insist on what the group drinker is indifferent to: taste. The look into the wallet or purse is therefore of secondary importance. On the contrary: They always get to know new, fantastic beers. They give a sense to their life. They have long since said good-bye to the demand: Man is supposed to drink three liters per day, which is misunderstood by group drinkers as in their translation it means *guzzling* three liters (if three are sufficient enough?).

Beer friends interpret this demand as follows: Man should *enjoy* three liters per day. That is what it comes down to. Life should not be passed over and done with by a rash execution of simple basic human needs just in order to survive but *lived*, with quality.

As the beer connoisseurs are still a distinct minority (and will remain so for a long time), they are often sneered at by remarks like "What kind of piss are drinking there?" or "Is this stuff drinkable at all?" Remarks which provoke beer connoisseurs to the connotation: "These kids are never going to grow up."

Beer is good for the health. You can find every type of vitamin in it (apart from C). So the amount is important, plus an apple or a pear. That does not apply to group beer. At the bottom line it is rather detrimental to health as it fulfills the requirements of the German Purity Law only marginally and requires the human body to get used to something which originally did not belong to the master plan of human evolution.

Group drinkers of old age are only seldom encountered. Aged group drinkers who enjoy good health are those who gave up their "group-drinking career" in time and have *involuntarily changed sides* to something else involuntarily, as craft beer drinking unfortunately never happened in their personal life and remained therefore unknown. Often the stop-gap became the infamous glass of red wine. Craft beer drinkers enjoy in old age *their beer*, too.

Additionally, to the classifications including all comments given, it should be said that the special skill of the beer connoisseur to appreciate a blitz beer and its derived species is something the group drinker completely lacks. It takes a basic understanding of what a *real* beer is – knowledge which can exclusively attributed only to the beer friend who knows that beer, is not the same as *beer.*

4 Demarcations

Beer and friendship don't mix! An axiom which is not normally examined closely enough but how true it is. Beer connoisseurs know that beer is either industrially or non-industrially brewed. Industrially brewed beer is also called group beer because it belongs to groups (corporations) which have divided up the market among themselves. "You wan' a group?" is translated like "You wan' (as an example) a *Sterni* (for Sternburger Beer)?" You could also ask: "Will you have a GB, too?" (similar to the abbreviated term PU for Pilsner Urquell). With group beer or GB it is *de facto* impossible to spoil one's friendship. Group Beer drinkers have a lot of other problems to cope with. Friendship is none of them.

Group beer connects in another way. It symbolizes *who* you are. It is a status symbol. Young people, mostly students, demonstrate their "brilliance" by carrying (in Germany) a *Sterni* in their hand for everyone to see, which they ration over a preferably long period of time. As it comes down to showing it, they *make a* perfectly clear *show* of their "beer".

Quality is in such a context almost insignificant – in addition they lack quality experience because of their youth – but also group beer drinkers try to define distinctive features. It is possible to enhance one's status by *showing a Becks* which is a bit dearer.

Regardless of quarrels as to which group beer is status-wise the best, the bottom line is that enjoying one's beer does not occupy their centre stage. Another phenomenon which substantiates the above-said is the fact that the sales figures unequivocally speak for the industry beer. How is that possible?

An experiment in a typical liquor supermarket proved that GB (group Beer) drinkers pass the craft beer section, actually without noticing it. Basically the GB drinker lets himself only be guided by the price. On entering the shop his head is bound upwards. What he is actually doing is looking at the price tags hanging from the ceiling. That is the first thing he sees.

The moment he finds the lowest-priced beer, he starts comparing it with the other (discount) prices. If he notes that his GB is not among them, he will start screaming and ranting, insulting the corporation because of its rip-off practices.

These beer drinkers are pleased the moment they see the word beer on the bottle's label to be sure that what they are about to buy is really beer. Popular group beers are *Radeberger, Lübzer, Krombacher, Warsteiner, Becks, Berliner Kindl* and *Hasseröder*, virtually, nearly everything that can be found in every common liquor shop or supermarket.

The decisive factors for GB drinkers are symbolism and low price. The beer connoisseur does not let himself be fooled by the fact that the groups make sure that their beers get all kinds of awards, medals and prizes. It gives beer friends something to chuckle about when the corporation decorates its best *Schultheiss* corner pub in Berlin. Fantasy literature would call it a paradox. In real life it is absurdly **too** real.

Is it possible to have a blitz with a GB? **Absolutely not!** Understanding this criteria is no problem for beer friends. Among GB drinkers a "blitz beer" might be in existence, too, but it drives towards something different. "You'll manage a last one, pal" intended as a question or a statement, is their meaning of "blitz beer". The GB drinker still has enough energy *and money* to afford a last beer. That *"You'll manage a last one, pal"* solely leads to more recognition.

The dread of emerging boredom (because the pal is leaving) could be another motive for encouragement. "You can't go now and leave us like that, we haven't finished discussing our problem yet." It quickly becomes clear it is about everything else but the one important thing: enjoying truly good beer.

Therefore it is improbable that GB drinking could be connected to blitz beer drinking. A GB drinker will never have an emergency. Even if standing by a food stall and his bus is arriving, his GB will not turn automatically into a blitz beer, only because he suddenly finds himself in a hurry, guzzling his beer – as if it were his very last – only to get on the bus on time.

Naturally, GB drinkers meet up too – if they are not walking about somewhere, proudly displaying their much appreciated beer bottle, but here the core is not the joint beer pleasure but the killing of time, dawdling it away into oblivion. The meeting points are generally known and the main object to *cling to* is the bottle.

Often while talking, the participants gesticulate. By doing so, the GB drinker will give his behavior a certain degree of earnestness, though there is actually no such thing. A typical answer of the accosted whether he would like to have another beer is: "Yeah, bring me one."

As you have noticed, nothing is said about what sort of beer. The main thing is another bottle. This is typical behavior of GB drinkers. These often halfheartedly slurred statements are more important for them than the beverage. The question, of course, is if the accosted would have improved or worsened his situation quality-wise if he had disclosed a concrete sort of beer.

There are pubs in Berlin where you can have a bottled beer for one euro: *Sterni* or *Öttinger*. In such cases all words are superfluous, and it is clear: A craft beer cannot be obtained under such circumstances.

At this point it shall be noted that beer friends do not mind the massive advance of industry beer. They will not paint banners and campaign against it. As long as governments do not lawfully ban the brewing of craft beer and make brewing as well as beer consuming a punishable offence, the beer connoisseur will discreetly stay on the sidelines. He is going to enjoy his beer because he is in the know that drinking it can also bring considerable pleasure.

Almost clandestinely, more and more *black craft pearls* are coming into existence. The difference between GB and craft beer (CB) becomes better known, and by this, the number of beer connoisseurs has started rising ever so slightly, but beer friends do not have to be afraid of being interfered with by GB drinkers. The corporation will take care of that.

The danger that the groups see the craft beer breweries as a thorn in their sides will not be removed by that. Should the danger for craft beer become all too real, what is left is perhaps the English way: the foundation of an organization for saving real beer (as in England the CAMRA: CAMpaign for Real Ale).

Beer friends can be protected by putting GBs on the black list in special liquor shops and quality restaurants, i.e. they are not available in general. This would keep the GB drinkers at bay. It is simply important that no mixing up occurs. It would be the same with human beings who from now on would be paired with penguins. That would also be absurd.

There is a recent case where the proprietor of a craft beer sales point tried to scare away GB drinkers by putting up a huge *Sternburg* plastic beer bottle in the penalty corner of his shop, clearly visible from the entrance, and sending out a warning to all – as if the end of the world was impending if beer friends stopped preserving *their beer*.

Naturally, group beer will not be able to harm beer friends as they avoid it out of natural instinct. "Would you drink a *Hasseröder* in the middle of the Sahara if nothing else to drink were available?" The beer friend would have to drink it in order to survive, but he would not contemplate it as beer and look forward to it.

For him it would be nothing else but a liquid which helps him survive, and he would not waste another thought on it. Quite different the GB drinker: "Oh my, if this isn't a yummy *Hasseröder*, and in the middle of the Sahara!" Sure enough, for him it would be whoopee in the first place, for the beer connoisseur only a mirage.

At this point it shall be made clear again that a beer which aims at being quaffed in one go is not a blitz beer in its classical sense. Even when the respected person had to suffer from extreme thirst (because of dehydration) over a long period of time!

It may well be that the circumstances – because of time pressure – do not permit to drink a beer in another way than in one go. It would not make sense to sit down first if the beer glass had already been emptied before reaching the working top of the table. It is correct if you say a blitz is consumed in a relatively swift way. But in the end *like a flash* and *the pleasure of a blitz beer* are poles apart.

A beer drinker is not automatically a GB drinker. The problem lies therein that a GB drinker has *never looked over the rim of his bottle,* that he has been pleased with what he found, and had, or that he has never heard about beers with taste. In other words: He has been living under a rock. It is especially tragic for those who happily reach the age of retirement and suddenly discover real beer – craft beer.

There is quite some pep talk necessary to stop the never-ending sea of tears. Better late than never! Beer friends are not averse to latecomers. On the contrary, they are glad to know all who are able to lay down their prejudices and take part in the pleasure presented by real beer.

A question often asked is: Can singles also become blitz beer drinkers? Basically, yes, although rather seldom. Naturally, also singles have an important, unpostponable appointment occasionally (the start of work is not meant by that). Beer friends who are single will therefore not brag with it. They will stay on the sidelines and be content with a finish beer, what makes sense.

Repetition: The thought of competition is utterly alien to beer friends. Blitz beer is a matter of spontaneity. What kind of spontaneity shall arise for singles to get into a blitz beer situation? Even the most hard-boiled single would start shrugging his shoulders at such an idea.

5 Prospects

For beer connoisseurs the future of beer can be described as looking quite bright. Really quite different from the GB drinkers who march toward hard times, as if the contours on the bottle label start to blur and the word beer becomes more and more illegible.

The corporations are now trying new tricks, e.g. by giving their bottle labels retro looks with nice pictures, hoping to retain their customers. But group drinkers feel themselves driven into the corner by something else: through constant price increases, so that remarks like "What am I to do without my *Schultheiss?*" or "Then there will be nothing left to live on." can be heard more often than before.

Whilst the beer friend usually informs about where he can drink another tasty drop someplace else or where a new micro brewery has opened its gates – the trend is continuously rising – the poor *Sterni* man has to turn his purse inside out all the time and scrape his last cents out of its chafed leather wrinkles.

In the future he will additionally have to convince himself if that what he is holding in his hand can still be counted as what is still defined under the term "beer". How lucky we are (think the group managers), that they let their market researchers fan out and who are now about to record their latest ideas to be able to *keep* (with the practical realization of these ideas) their most faithful customers *in line* or in other words *keep them in their group.*

This is something which does not bother the CB brewer. He would send some of his newest ideas to a beer tasting, at which enough expert people take part, and the rest goes without saying. One thing is clear, the moment the small breweries and the beer shops get a better grip on logistics, then more and more *craft beer sales points* are going to be set up.

By this method, the way to the "beer well" is going to get shorter for many a beer friend. You would think that the idea of having a blitz – yes or no? – will take a backseat, but you've got the cart before the horse here. Blitz beer will gain in importance because emergencies will loom ahead less unrelentingly. Beer friends will get bolder, as the way from their pleasure points to their homes will become shorter and therefore easier to manage. So a blitz here and there could indeed be taken into account.

What beer friends cannot stand is practicing blitz beer drinking on the sly at home. Many a man thinks that he can – by way of being able to do so – make an impression on other beer friends, but such a person would have to get used to living in the shadows, and this for a long time, if he has been found out. Once again it shall be repeated that the opportunity for a blitz arises spontaneously, and spontaneity cannot be practiced. It always looks like as if you tried but failed, and it is conspicuous in addition. So please, don't do that at home! You're better off taking care of your women.

Blitz beer is not going to lose its significance, even though the conscious beer friend will not exclusively devote his free time to enjoying a good beer. Amongst experts the talk is predominantly about an "insertion" such as: "Yep, I have just inserted an hour, but then I'll have to leave again."

Beer friends have private and social commitments en masse which they are expected to fulfill unconditionally. They are omnifariously involved in society, and working life and they do not go guzzling, even if it appears to be so on occasions. Even then a special kind of beer pleasure is not expected, or the beer friend simply has succumbed to it. Heads are shaken sympathetically if such an escapade happens to a beer friend. As a rule such an incident is unusual and only repeats itself at wide intervals. There is no reason to worry. Besides, the quality of the beer provides everything else to upend the "sinner" quickly. That can be depended on.

Beer friends are not escapists who have to cloister themselves away. The fact alone, that they are able to drink finish and blitz beers, shows clearly that they have both feet on the ground and can be relied on.

When their day ends, they are of sound mind and with their heads on straight. It is never about finding out how much beer one can drink, or to say it in other words, guzzling till the doctor comes. Such experiments are ceded, with head held high, to the group drinker. The beer connoisseur readily waives such tournaments.

Beer friends do not have a devil-may-care attitude, they think of the coming generations, too. They want the good old beer tradition not to *decline like the Roman Empire* but to continue to belong to the common things of daily life in the future as well as today. Every source of help is welcome. The craft beer sales points alone succeed in demonstrating their high quality beer that is on offer and "converting" many a group drinker to the true faith in beer. As a result, usually, words of thanks can be heard for weeks on end.

At this point another important tip shall be revealed. There are beer drinkers in the world who do not only appreciate their beer but also like to describe the taste of it at length: so-called *tickers*. The uninitiated often get the impression of having lost themselves in a prize competition or a bingo night.

Tickers are able to describe the beer they have consumed, perfectly and recognizably. Expert tickers claim of themselves to be able to exactly "taste" the beers they had about twenty years ago and recognize them immediately still today.

What is my point? A ticker is unfamiliar with the term blitz beer. He simply does not have the balls to face up to it. That would be contrary to his nature. With him there is the *last sip of the day* at max. Therefore tickers should not be involved in blitz beer discussions in order to avoid destroying or distorting their own conception of their world of beer.

Are women able to drink a blitz? This is of course possible, but as rare as the Blue Mauritius. Women basically differ in their drinking behavior from men. It is really different: after one or two beers they draw the line. Women do not intend to be competition to their men folk. After a third they are mostly crocked anyway; their legs straddle apart, meaning, they are going their own ways. In such moments women desperately clutch at something to hold on. Therefore: no. No way! A blitz would only make them look helpless. Let alone a super blitz. A level-headed publican would not let such a silliness come up in the first place.

6 Recommendations

Regarding beer recommendations, we give here only those which are special and suitable for a blitz beer. (Once again the advice: A decision for a half liter could be daring and is more or less reserved only for the experienced blitz beer drinker.) The sorts named hereafter are to be considered as a very small selection of those a blitz beer drinker would choose from.

A) From bottles:

- 0.5 liters

a) Pottensteiner Vollbier

b) Mönchsambacher Lager

c) Goldener Schlüssel (Alt)

d) Uerige (Alt)

e) Füchschen (Alt)

f) Waldhaus Pils

g) Moritz Fiege Pils

h) Weiherer Kellerbier

i) Krug-Bräu Lager

j) Huppendorfer Vollbier

- 0.33 liters

a) Amarsi (IPA)

b) Wedding Pale Ale

c) Schoppe XPA

d) Hop Gun (IPA)

e) Waldhaus Pils

f) Sierra Nevada Torpedo

g) Laguna

h) Schönramer IPA

It is not possible to imagine these beer types without their seasonal ones – beers which can only be obtained for a short or specific time.

To those belong beers like:

a) Märzen of Camba

b) Weihnachtsfestbiere like of Krug-Bräu.

B) From nearly all German in-house breweries: (comp. www.hausbrauerei.de):

As special recommendations only a few pearls shall be named here representatively:

a) Meierei in Potsdam

b) Forsthaus in Potsdam

c) Eschenbräu in Berlin

d) Papiermühle in Jena

e) Feierling in Freiburg

f) Füchschen in Düsseldorf

g) Uerige in Düsseldorf

h) Kieler Brewery

i) Am Waldschlösschen in Dresden

j) Schupke in Berlin-Wittenau

7 Blitz (Beer) Elsewhere

If you start researching the internet, you will have some hits regarding blitz beer. You will soon understand that the term varies and has different interpretations.

In 2003 there were several entries, among them a discussion what a blitz beer could be. "Let's go for a blitz beer." At first, people thought it had something to do with England because of the opening hours. There was even a question if it be something to do with "blitzkrieg". There was a considerable uncertainty. "A fast pint" or "a quickie", these were mostly the answers.

Blitz beer was connected to "drinking contest" as the pubs in England would close shop at eleven. The best answer I found was: "… but I think I'd better use another word."

Quite right. If you do not know something accurately, you should keep your mouth shut. Quite clearly, because everybody who strove for an obvious answer failed completely – in other words – "missed the target by miles". Where these basic approaches stem from – or the courage to dare a definition - has already been depicted quite extensively above.

The conclusion is: You cannot go for a blitz beer. Another author has propounded that blitz beer could be understood as "Let's get pissed" what actually means as he correctly explains: "… to be pissed by eleven, you have to toss them down in a quick succession." A mathematician would say at this point: quod erat demonstrandum (which had to be demonstrated). No further comments necessary.

There is another situation, i.e. if the bill is being paid or has already been paid after a snug evening in the restaurant, and "**it**" is coming over the beer friend: His heart demands another beer. Yielding to his heart, he tells his woman: "I'll just have a blitz beer."

What do we have here? Quite clearly, it is about an additional beer, plain and simple about a so-called extended finish beer. The term blitz beer was solely used to soothe the woman and signalize to her that it will not take long as logically the ignoramus would associate blitz beer with something especially fast, like a flash, but you can only call it a blitz beer if there is an important event ahead the attendance of which cannot be cancelled and the remaining time has become extremely tight.

A Blitzo will be able to factor this tight time frame in, and control it. The question is: Will the above-mentioned beer friend be able to *convince* his woman that there is still enough time for a blitz.

Another phenomenon which you can find on the internet is the explanation of "rapid tapping". So to say:

as an athletic contest. It is not about the beer but the *dexterity of tapping*. The headline *There is Blitz Beer Being Served on Schalke* is therefore complete nonsense. *How fast are the Berliners at Tapping Beer?* the headline continues. (By the way, the Schalke record for a freshly tapped beer is now set at three minutes, ready to be served. "The lightning-fast three-minute Pils", they proudly announce blowing their own trumpets.) If I quickly "tap" soda pop, it will not turn into a blitz soda, otherwise we would soon have a Blitz-OJ and blitz milk etc.

"Let's blitz it up, pal!" we would soon hear everywhere. That's as pointless as "lightning-fast blitz beer". But we are getting off track here and digressing. The beer friend repudiates every athletic innuendo, including *one arm snatching in the half liter class*.

Pleasure and sports do not mix whilst having a beer, they just do not fit together. This may work smoothly with group beer, but not with craft beer. The inhabitants of Munich should fetch the tapsters from Schalke to their tent city, then perhaps even more money would start rolling in.

You can also find a 2006 entry on the internet about the interesting term "siege blitz beer". Unfortunately, no explanation was given as to what the term implies. Only locations like Israel and Jordan were mentioned.

Meanwhile a lot of attempts are being made to place the word beer in names of beer. The brewery in Berlin-Spandau serves a seasonal POTZ-BLITZ-BIER every year, a Vollbier (style: Octoberfest/Maerzen) with 14% original wort and 5.8 ABV. The blitz is meant to indicate something *strong*, like a kick (which, alas, many a drinker missed).

In Münsterland, in Oelde, there is the brewery Potts which offers POTT'S BLITZ in the flavours, elder and lime-ginger, a non-alcoholic wheat mix.

In Brazil, Pato Branco, there (possibly) is still the BLITZ BREWERY in existence which offer(ed) a BLITZ DOPPELBOCK.

Basically, the blitz is used picture-wise or symbolically as a marketing tool. Beer strikes like lightning. The English-speaking area has several names for which the term blitz is used on the label.

English words for blitz are *flash, bolt* and *lightning.* There is the *Bolt Low Carb Lager* of Dan Murphy's in Australia, or the pale ale lager *Thunderbolt Superstrong* of the brewery Mount Shivalik in India, or the *Clockwork Thunder & Lightning* of Mac Lay's in Glasgow, Scotland, or *Flash*-Beers from San Diego, United States.

Also in brewery names you can find the term blitz. In North Carolina there is the *Bolt Brewery* to be opened in spring 2014. Then there is the *Lightning Brewery* in San Diego. Also in San Diego you can find the *Green Flash Brewing Company.* Or those who could do with *thunder* (instead of blitz) can go and see the *Thunder*

Canyon Brewery in Tucson, which has been in existence for more than fifteen years now. There are no indications that these flashes would have caused casualties (on account of their dreaded lightning impact).

After that the blitz party seems to be over. No blitz anymore, far and wide - but perhaps soon there will be more. If you find a flash on the label of a bottle, do not confuse it with blitz beer. Of course, the blitz alone can be a very fine vehicle for advertising.

8 Glossary